A Short, Illustrated History of...

SCIENTIFIC DISCOVERIES

Clive Gifford   Rita Petruccioli

T0390591

ROSEN
PUBLISHING

Published in 2025 by The Rosen Publishing Group, Inc.
2544 Clinton Street, Buffalo, NY 14224

First published in Great Britain in 2020 by The Watts Publishing Group
Copyright © The Watts Publishing Group, 2020

Series Editor: Amy Pimperton
Series Designer: Lisa Peacock
Illustrations by Rita Petruccioli

Cataloging-in-Publication Data

Names: Gifford, Clive, author. | Petruccioli, Rita, illustrator.
Title: Scientific discoveries / by Clive Gifford, illustrated by Rita Petruccioli.
Description: Buffalo, New York : Rosen Publishing, 2025. | Series: A short, illustrated history of... | Includes glossary and index.
Identifiers: ISBN 9781499476484 (pbk.) | ISBN 9781499476491 (library bound) | ISBN 9781499476507 (ebook)
Subjects: LCSH: Science–History–Juvenile literature. | Discoveries in science–History–Juvenile literature.
Classification: LCC Q126.4 G56 2025 | DDC 509–dc23

Manufactured in the United States of America

CPSIA Compliance Information: Batch #CSRYA25.
For further information, contact Rosen Publishing, New York, New York, at 1-800-237-9932.

Find us on

Contents

Dreaming of Discoveries

People have always wondered how the world works. Over thousands of years, curiosity has led to huge amounts of new knowledge. Scientists dream of making a major discovery, coming up with a new idea that explains how something works or finding something that no one has seen before.

Prehistoric people made important discoveries that improved their lives. These included what plants were good or harmful to eat and how to make fire and use it to cook food or heat metals to make useful tools. Ancient peoples made discoveries through experimenting with objects and materials.

The ancient Romans found that adding volcanic ash to cement made a super-strong type of concrete. Many Roman structures built with this 2,000-year-old concrete, such as the Pantheon in Rome, Italy, still stand to this day.

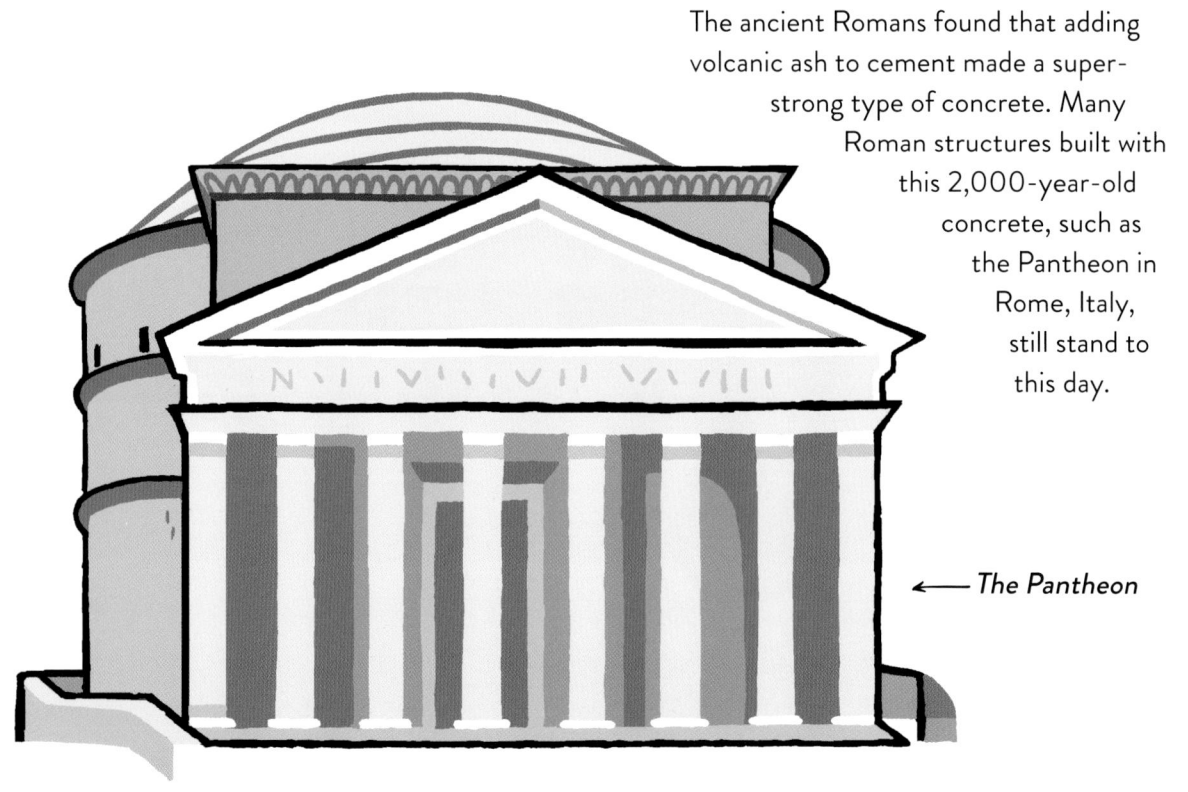

←— *The Pantheon*

Discoveries have shaped what we know about ourselves and how our bodies work. They have also taught us much about other living things both now and in the past, and about the planet we all live on. Many important discoveries, such as those made by astronomer and physicist Galileo Galilei (1564–1642), have helped us gain a sense of our place in space and what the universe consists of beyond Earth.

Galileo Galilei ⟶

Some discoveries come about due to a single flash of inspiration (see Archimedes on pages 8–9) or through a lucky accident. X-rays (see pages 34–35) began with an accidental discovery. In contrast, many discoveries can take years or decades of hard work. Contained in this book are examples of many different scientific discoveries that have all had a major impact on the world.

Center of Attention

For thousands of years people looked up and noted how the stars moved through the night sky throughout the year. Most, including ancient Greek astronomer Claudius Ptolemy (c. CE 100–c. 170), assumed that Earth stood still at the center of the universe and all the stars and planets revolved about it. This is known as the geocentric model. Ptolemy's *Almagest* (written around CE 150) was held as fact by most people for almost 1,500 years.

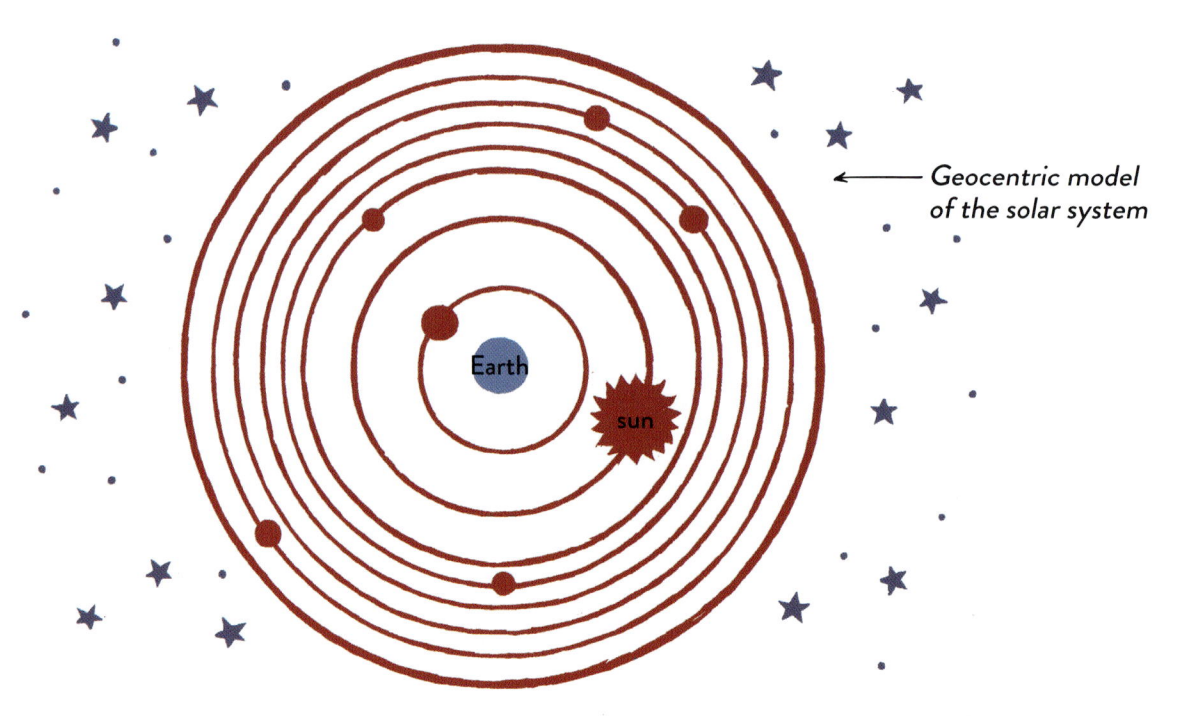

Geocentric model of the solar system

Hundreds of years before Ptolemy, another ancient Greek, Aristarchus of Samos (c. 310–c. 230 BCE), came up with a different idea. He believed that only the moon orbited Earth and that our planet and all the other planets traveled around the sun on circular paths (we now know the paths are oval-shaped). This is known as the heliocentric model.

Aristarchus's ideas were largely forgotten about until Polish astronomer Nicolaus Copernicus (1473–1543) published a book in 1543. Called *On The Revolutions of the Heavenly Spheres*, it stated that Earth spins around its own axis, creating the days, while at the same time traveling around the sun on a long path called an orbit. Each complete orbit equals a year. Copernicus also thought that the size of each planet's orbit depends on how far away it is from the sun.

Earth

sun

Copernicus →
and the
heliocentric
model of the
solar system

Controversy

Copernicus's ideas were revolutionary to many and, in 1616, the powerful Catholic Church banned the book for over 200 years because it was at odds with the idea that God placed man at the center of the universe. Astronomers and scientists, such as Johannes Kepler (1571–1630) and Isaac Newton (1642–1727), found that Copernicus (and Aristarchus before him) was largely correct. Today, we know that it takes Earth 365.25 days to complete its journey around the sun.

Eureka!

Archimedes (c. 287–c. 212 BCE) was born in the Greek city-state of Syracuse on the island of Sicily. He was a mathematical and mechanical genius. He studied in Alexandria, Egypt, but later returned home.

He was one of the first scientists to investigate how simple machines worked, such as levers, pulleys, and screws, and he invented many helpful machines. These included block and tackles, which combine many pulleys together to lift heavy loads. He also invented the screw pump — a hollow tube with a screw inside. When turned, the screw raised water from deep rivers or lakes. Today the devices are often used to move powders and grains, as well as liquids.

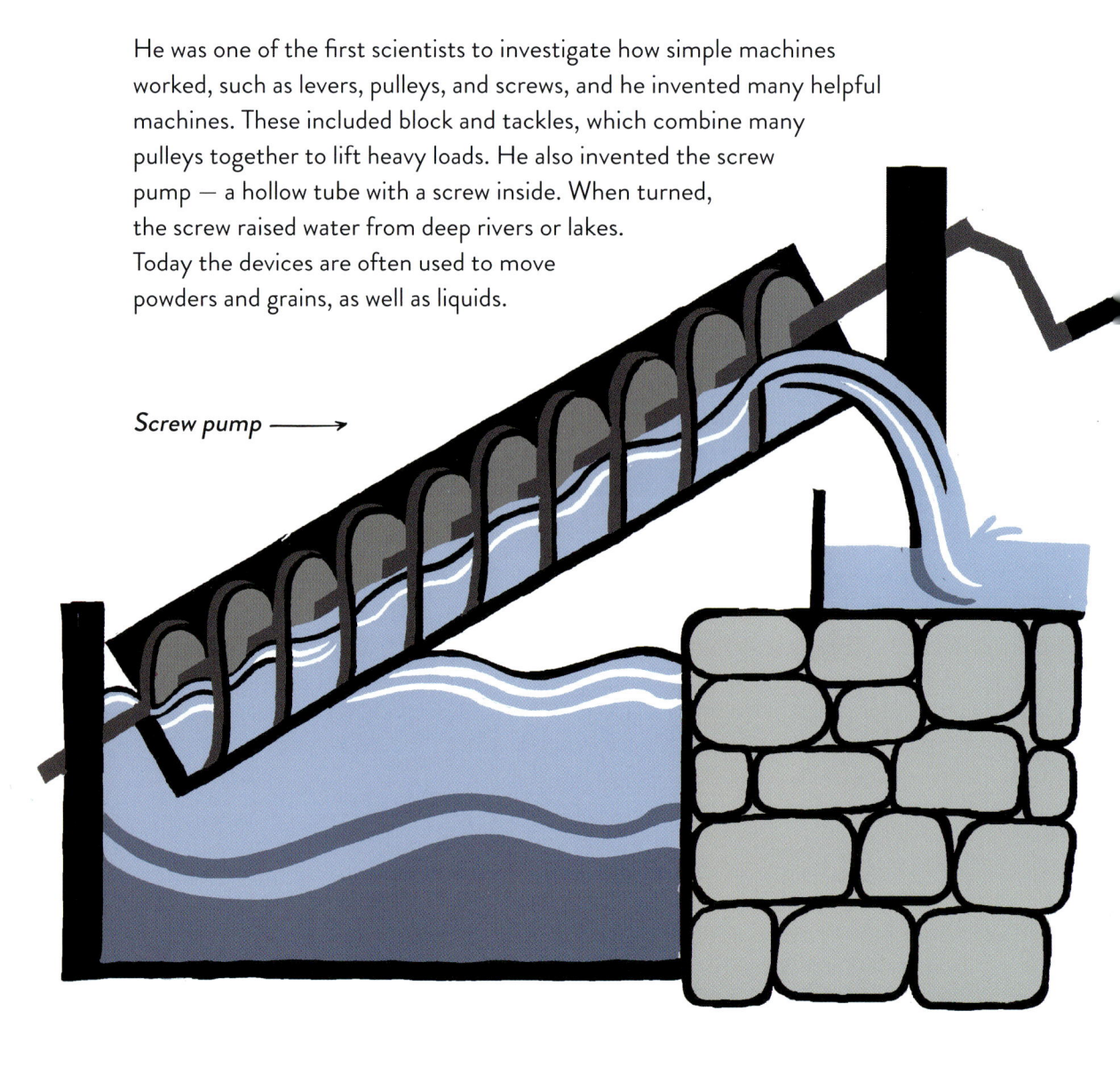

Screw pump ⟶

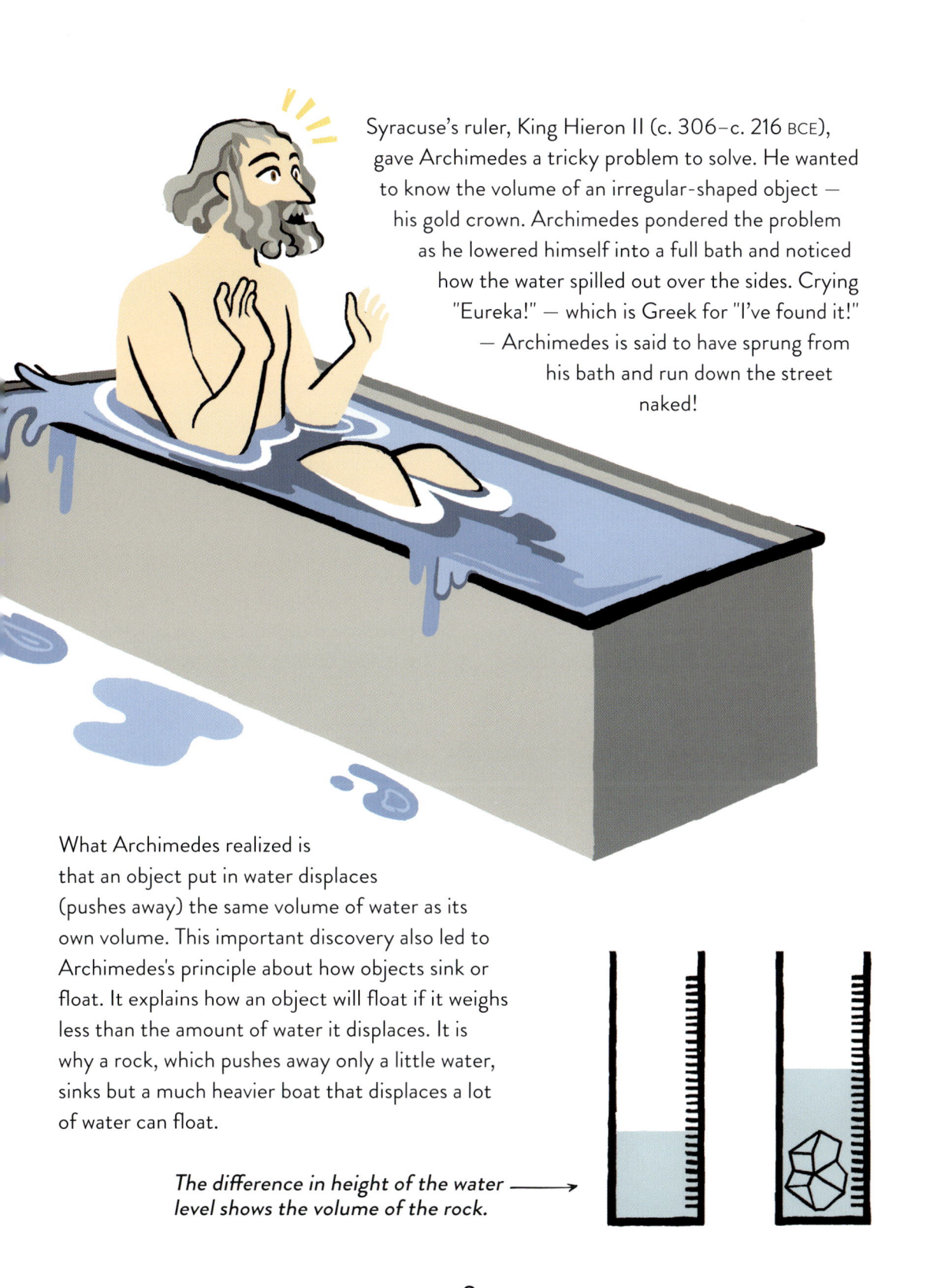

Syracuse's ruler, King Hieron II (c. 306–c. 216 BCE), gave Archimedes a tricky problem to solve. He wanted to know the volume of an irregular-shaped object — his gold crown. Archimedes pondered the problem as he lowered himself into a full bath and noticed how the water spilled out over the sides. Crying "Eureka!" — which is Greek for "I've found it!" — Archimedes is said to have sprung from his bath and run down the street naked!

What Archimedes realized is that an object put in water displaces (pushes away) the same volume of water as its own volume. This important discovery also led to Archimedes's principle about how objects sink or float. It explains how an object will float if it weighs less than the amount of water it displaces. It is why a rock, which pushes away only a little water, sinks but a much heavier boat that displaces a lot of water can float.

The difference in height of the water level shows the volume of the rock.

A Microscopic World

Microscopes were invented in the 16th century by placing two lenses in a tube to make small objects appear bigger. By 1660, some microscopes could magnify objects more than 100 times. English scientist Robert Hooke (1635–1703) used such microscopes to study the natural world. He discovered how plants are made up of individual building blocks, which he named cells.

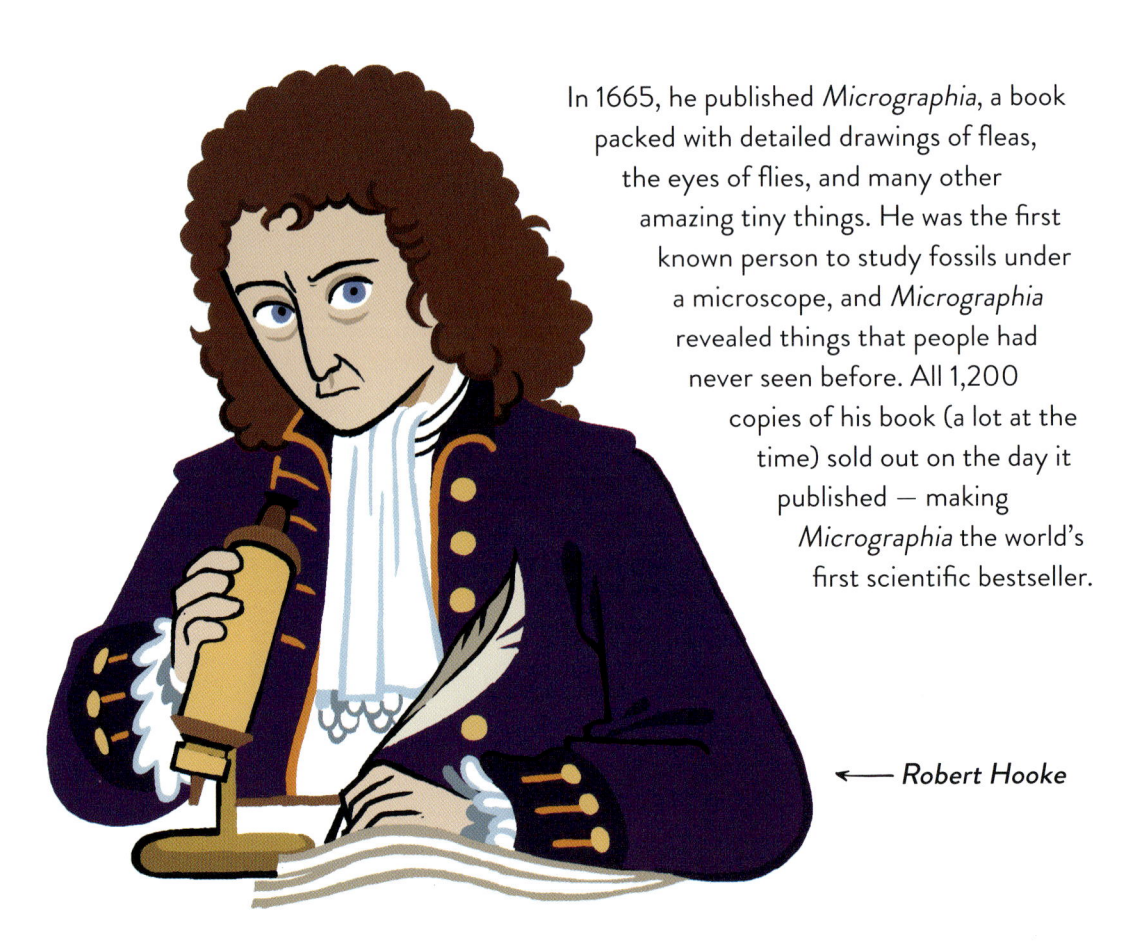

In 1665, he published *Micrographia*, a book packed with detailed drawings of fleas, the eyes of flies, and many other amazing tiny things. He was the first known person to study fossils under a microscope, and *Micrographia* revealed things that people had never seen before. All 1,200 copies of his book (a lot at the time) sold out on the day it published — making *Micrographia* the world's first scientific bestseller.

← *Robert Hooke*

Dutch merchant Antonie van Leeuwenhoek (1632–1723) visited London in 1668, saw Hooke's book, and was fascinated. He returned home and started making lenses and microscopes — in secret at first. He proved to be expert at the task and is thought to have made over 500 microscopes. Some had a tiny single lens the size of a pinhole but could magnify objects up to 270 times.

Antonie van Leeuwenhoek ⟶

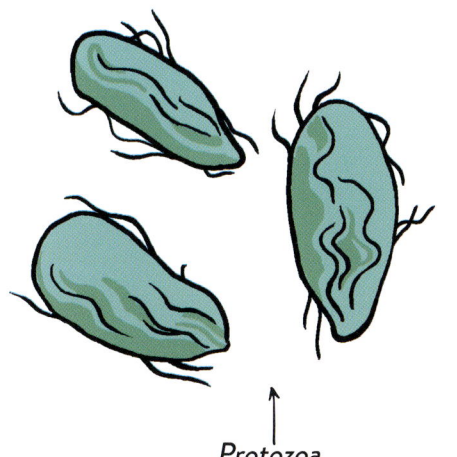

↑
Protozoa

Using his microscopes, van Leeuwenhoek discovered single-celled living things called protozoa, as well as bacteria in water and tiny microbes living on the human body and in plaque between teeth. He let lice breed on his legs to observe them and left his feet unwashed to study the microbes that lived in the dirt between his toes! He was the first to see the living individual sperm of animals and to describe blood cells in detail.

Gravity

In 1665, Isaac Newton fled Cambridge University due to a plague epidemic. He retreated to his family's farm in Lincolnshire for almost two years. There, he discovered the force of attraction between objects, which he called gravity. Newton's law of universal gravitation explained how gravity works and how it applies throughout the universe.

Newton defined gravity as an invisible pulling force that works across space. It gets weaker the farther apart objects are but can still work over huge distances. All objects exert some gravity, and Newton realized that the more mass (material) an object has, the more gravity it has. The sun, for example, is so massive that its gravity pulls Earth into an orbit around it, even though the two objects are over 92 million miles (149 million km) apart.

Earth's gravity causes objects thrown into the air to fall back to the ground. Our planet's gravity is also strong enough to keep the moon from whizzing off into space. In return, the moon's gravity acts on Earth, pulling the waters of the seas and oceans to form tides.

Falling Apples

The story goes that Newton discovered gravity when observing apples falling from a tree at his home. Whether this is true or not, Newton's work was certainly inspired by observing the world around him.

Newton published his work in his 1687 book, *Philosophiæ Naturalis Principia Mathematica*, which caused a sensation. It explained for the first time how planets and moons moved through space and changed how people looked at the universe.

Weighty Matters

Earth's gravity gives objects their weight. On planets with less gravity, you would weigh less, and on massive planets with more gravity, you would weigh more. A 110-pound (50-kg) person on Earth, for example, would weigh about 42 lbs (19 kg) on Mars and 280 lbs (127 kg) on Jupiter.

Understanding Light

People originally thought that colors in light were a mixture of white light and darkness. In 1672, Isaac Newton announced the results of experiments he'd performed using glass blocks called prisms.

Light passed through a prism refracts (bends), and a range of colors appear. Newton identified seven: red, orange, yellow, green, blue, indigo, and violet. He called the range of colors a spectrum. These occur in nature when raindrops sometimes act as prisms, turning sunlight into a rainbow.

Isaac Newton studies the spectrum of visible light produced by a prism

Some scientists thought that the prism itself created the colors, but Newton proved them wrong. He reversed the process, shining all the colors back onto another prism, where they formed white light, proving that light is a combination of all the colors. Scientists later learned that light travels in waves and each color has its own wavelength. When they travel through a prism, each wavelength refracts a different amount, which is why they separate out.

Around the same time, a Danish astronomer named Ole Rømer (1644–1710) was studying the moons of Jupiter. He noticed that his observations of one moon, called Io, varied depending on how close Earth and Jupiter were to each other. These variations could be used to figure out how fast light travels. At the time, no one had a clear idea of the speed of light.

Ole Rømer

Jupiter ⟶

Speed of Light

Using Rømer's observations, in 1676 Dutch scientist Christiaan Huygens (1629–95) calculated light's speed as over 125,000 miles (201,168 km) every second — that's 300 times around the Earth in a minute! Later calculations showed that light actually travels even faster, at 186,282 miles (299,792 km) per second.

Elementary Discoveries

A chemical element is a substance, such as oxygen, gold, or carbon, that cannot be broken down into simpler substances. Some elements, particularly metals like iron, copper, and gold, were discovered thousands of years ago, but by 1700, only 13 elements were known.

The first element to be found using chemistry was phosphorus, by amateur German alchemist Hennig Brand (c. 1630–c. 1695 or c. 1710). He discovered it in 1679. He was heating urine, trying to become rich by turning it into gold, when he discovered a substance that he called "cold fire" because it glowed in the dark. The substance was the chemical element phosphorus. In the 19th century it was first used on match heads.

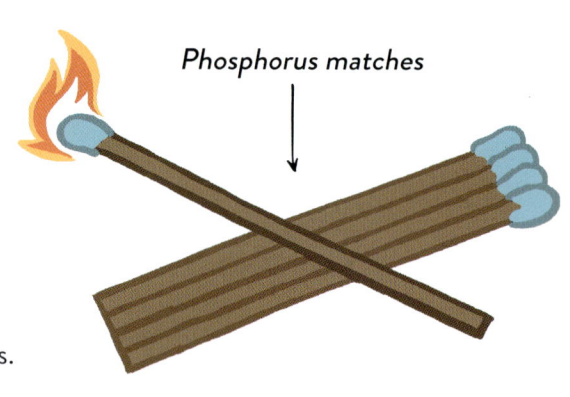

Phosphorus matches

← *Hennig Brand*

Many Elements

The ancient Greeks believed that everything in the world was made up of four elements: air, fire, earth, and water. We now know that none of those four are actually elements, but more than 90 elements exist naturally.

As chemistry advanced in the 18th and 19th centuries, a large number of elements were discovered. English chemist Humphry Davy (1778–1829) used the new invention of the voltaic pile electric battery (see pages 18–19) to split common substances, such as potash, into separate elements. In a busy two years (1807–08), he discovered potassium, sodium, and calcium. He also proved that chlorine and magnesium, which had both been discovered earlier, were also elements.

Splitting Up Substances

An atom is the smallest whole unit or particle of an element. In 1803, English chemist John Dalton (1766–1844) suggested that all matter is made up of atoms and all the atoms of one element are identical. Atoms are incredibly tiny — four million hydrogen atoms in a row would barely measure a single millimeter.

John Dalton ⟶

Electricity

In the 18th century, various scientists began experimenting with electricity. Many thought that lightning was made of electricity, but there were no safe methods to prove this. In 1752, Benjamin Franklin (1706–90) is said to have flown a kite during a thunderstorm to demonstrate the theory that lightning is made of electricity.

Franklin's kite is said to have had a metal wire attached to the top to attract lightning. A key tied to the kite's string was also connected to a glass jar (Leyden jar), which held the electricity. Whether he actually performed the experiment is not known for sure.

French physicist Thomas-François Dalibard (1709–78), who was aware of Franklin's theories, performed a similar experiment with a 40-foot-long (12 m) iron rod in 1752 (around a month before Franklin is said to have flown his kite). The rod drew electric sparks from a thunder cloud, proving Franklin right.

Franklin is said to have performed his kite experiment from the safety of a shed.

Italian scientist Alessandro Volta (1745–1827) discovered that particular chemical reactions could produce electricity. In 1800, Volta built a device called a voltaic pile from alternating discs of copper, zinc, and cardboard soaked in salty water. When both ends of the device were connected by wire, they formed a circuit. Chemical reactions between the disc materials created electricity, which flowed around the circuit. The voltaic pile was the first battery capable of producing a steady supply of electricity.

Voltaic piles and other new batteries were seized upon by scientists to experiment with. English scientist Michael Faraday (1791–1867) investigated links between electricity and magnetism, paving the way for electric motors. In 1831, he discovered how a coil of wire moving through a magnetic field induced (generated) an electric current in the wire. This vital principle became known as Faraday's law. Faraday built a machine he called a dynamo to demonstrate his new principle. Today, giant generators working on Faraday's principles produce huge amounts of electricity to light, heat, and power our homes and cities.

Michael Faraday

Extinction

Three hundred years ago, people thought that every type of plant and creature that ever lived on Earth was still alive and present. People couldn't believe that a god who created all things would allow any to be wiped out forever. Fossils were thought of as old remains of currently living things.

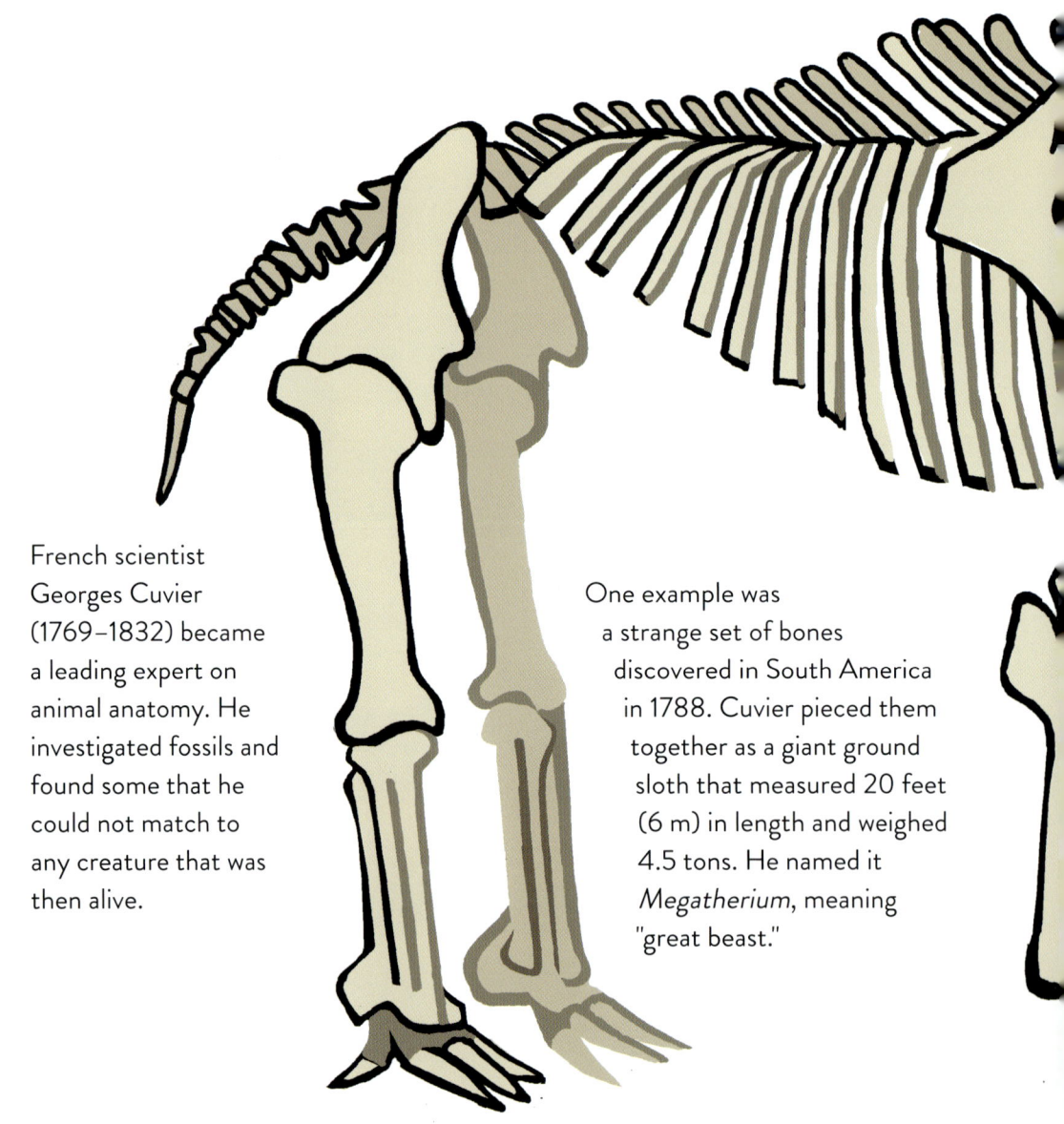

French scientist Georges Cuvier (1769–1832) became a leading expert on animal anatomy. He investigated fossils and found some that he could not match to any creature that was then alive.

One example was a strange set of bones discovered in South America in 1788. Cuvier pieced them together as a giant ground sloth that measured 20 feet (6 m) in length and weighed 4.5 tons. He named it *Megatherium*, meaning "great beast."

When examining what were thought to be elephant fossils from the U.S., Cuvier discovered that their bones and teeth were from a different species from the past, which he named mastodon. In 1800, he also studied and named the first known prehistoric flying reptile — the pterodactyl.

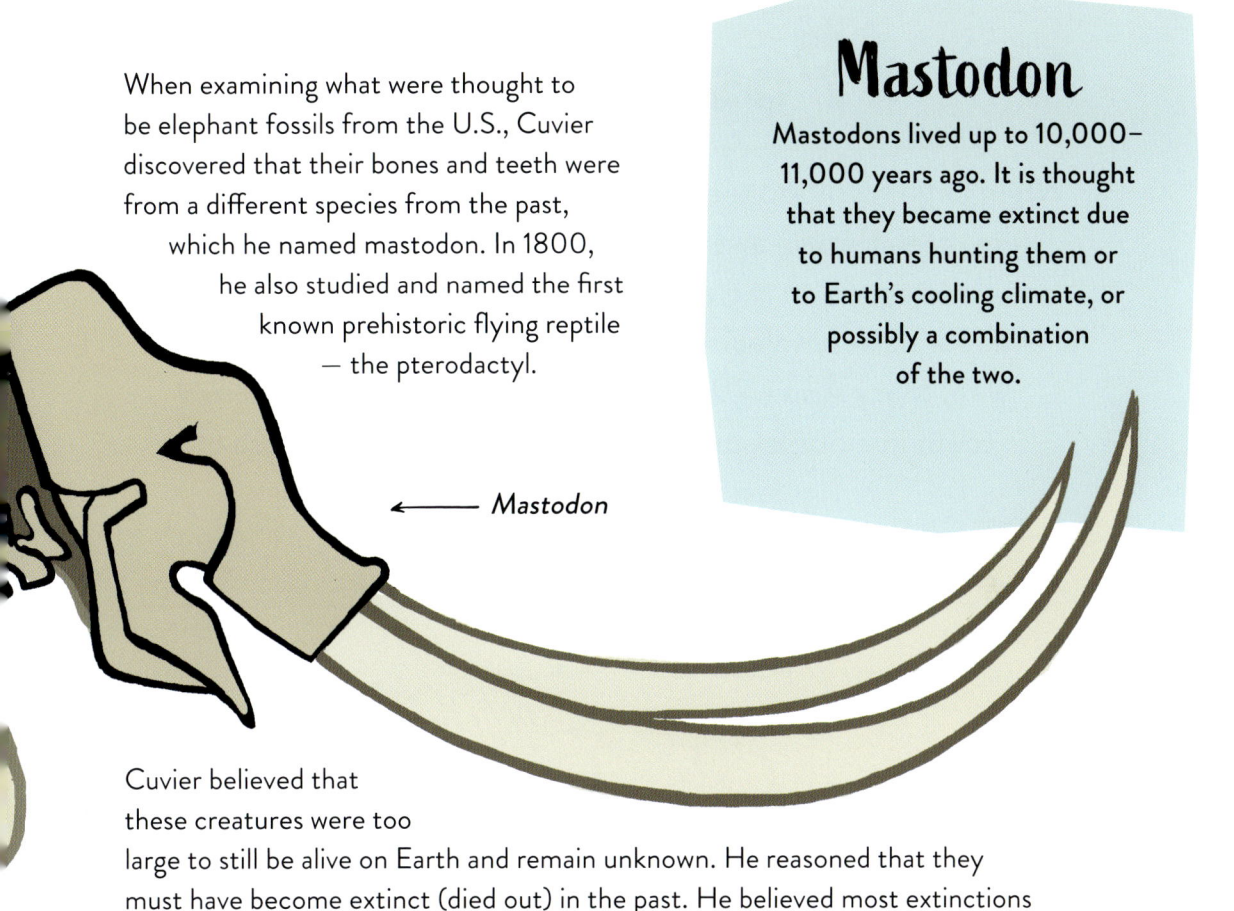

← Mastodon

Mastodon

Mastodons lived up to 10,000–11,000 years ago. It is thought that they became extinct due to humans hunting them or to Earth's cooling climate, or possibly a combination of the two.

Cuvier believed that these creatures were too large to still be alive on Earth and remain unknown. He reasoned that they must have become extinct (died out) in the past. He believed most extinctions came in waves caused by Earth going through sudden catastrophic changes.

Cuvier's theory of extinction shocked many people at the time but has been proven largely correct. Some scientists believe that most dinosaurs, along with three-quarters of all other animal species, died out around 65 million years ago after an asteroid crashed into Earth.

Mass Extinction Events

Five mass extinction events in Earth's history caused vast numbers of plants and animals to be wiped out. The most devastating was the Permian Extinction Event, which occurred between 299 and 252 million years ago. It caused the extinction of over 95 percent of marine species and around 70 percent of land species.

Fossil Finds

When large fossilised teeth or bones were found in the past, they were often thrown away or thought of as parts of giant people or even dragons. In the early 1820s, English country doctor and amateur palaeontologist Gideon Mantell (1790–1852) and his wife, Mary Ann (1795–1869), discovered giant, fossilized teeth in a Sussex quarry. The teeth looked like those of iguana lizards, only much larger.

Iguanodon fossil ⟶

Mantell figured out they were from a plant-eating giant reptile (up to 33 feet [10 m] in length), which no longer lived on Earth. He named it *Iguanodon*, and when bones of the creature were found, he and Mary Ann made sketches of what they thought it would have looked like. Mantell was the first to identify and describe fully a species of what we now call dinosaurs — prehistoric land reptiles that lived between 65 and 230 million years ago.

In 1832, Mantell discovered bones of the first heavily armored dinosaur, which he named *Hylaeosaurus*. Further discoveries followed all over the world, including *Stegosaurus* in 1876, *Diplodocus* in 1877, *Triceratops* in 1888, and *Tyrannosaurus rex* in 1902. Today, there are over 700 known species of dinosaur.

← *Tyrannosaurus rex*

Mary Anning

Combing the coast of Lyme Regis in Dorset, England, for seashells to sell, 12-year-old Mary Anning (1799–1847) discovered the 17-foot-long (5.2-m) skeleton of a mysterious creature in 1811. It was a prehistoric marine lizard called an ichthyosaur, which lived around 200 million years ago. Anning later discovered plesiosaurs and a prehistoric flying reptile called *Dimorphodon*. She also pioneered the study of dinosaur poop fossils, known as coprolites.

Theory of Evolution

In 1831, 22-year-old Charles Darwin (1809–82) sailed from England aboard HMS *Beagle* on a five-year around-the-world voyage of discovery. Darwin made notes and sketches and gathered samples of plants and creatures wherever the ship traveled. He collected fossils, saw how some were similar to living species he knew, and wondered how new species developed.

HMS *Beagle* ⟶

In 1835, the HMS *Beagle* moored at a group of Pacific Ocean islands called the Galápagos. Darwin noticed how creatures of the same species on each island differed in small ways. These differences are known as adaptations and help equip a living thing for survival. Darwin noted adaptations in birds called finches. The birds' beaks were all different shapes and sizes, depending on whether a bird's habitat was rich in fruit, seeds, leaves, or insects.

Returning home to England, his head full of questions, Darwin spent more than 20 years working on his ideas before his book, *On the Origin of Species*, was published in 1859. It explained how living things change over many generations to become new species — a process called evolution. Darwin also explained how adaptations in a species occur through something called natural selection. This is where members of a species best suited to their surroundings are more likely to survive and pass on their adaptations to their offspring.

← Charles Darwin

Evolving Beliefs

Darwin's ideas upset many who believed in a never-changing world created by God, but they eventually became widely accepted as an important part of science. The theory of evolution has helped change how we view the natural world.

Periodic Table

By the mid-19th century, over 60 chemical elements had been discovered (see pages 16–17), but their relationship to each other wasn't well understood. Dmitri Mendeleev (1834–1907) was a Russian science teacher who in 1855 decided to go back to school. He moved to St. Petersburg, studied hard, and eventually became a university professor of chemistry.

Mendeleev wrote down the names of the 63 known elements at the time, one per card. He added the key properties of each element on each card. Arranging the cards in columns and rows (known as periods) he noticed patterns forming. Columns of elements formed groups with similar properties. The left-most column, for instance, contained alkali metals that all reacted powerfully with water.

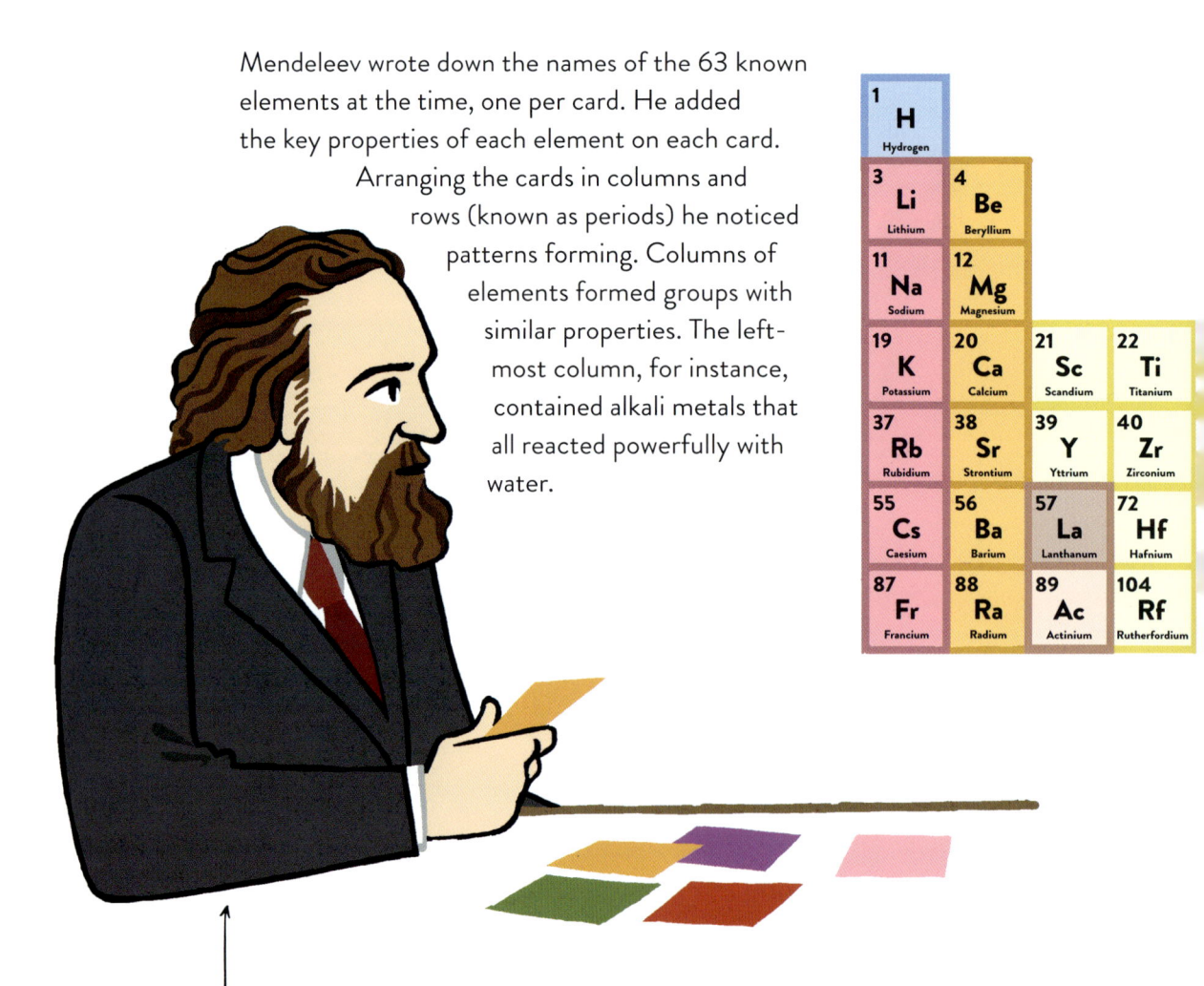

Dmitri Mendeleev

When Mendeleev first demonstrated his periodic table in 1869, he took a risk and left gaps for elements he proposed existed but had yet to be discovered. Using the rest of the table, he even predicted the properties these unknown elements might have.

The gaps attracted criticism from some scientists who were not convinced that his table was accurate. However, it did not take long for further discoveries to prove him right. In 1875, gallium was discovered by French chemist Paul-Émile Lecoq de Boisbaudran (1838–1912). It fit into a gap in Mendeleev's table. So did scandium in 1879 and germanium in 1885.

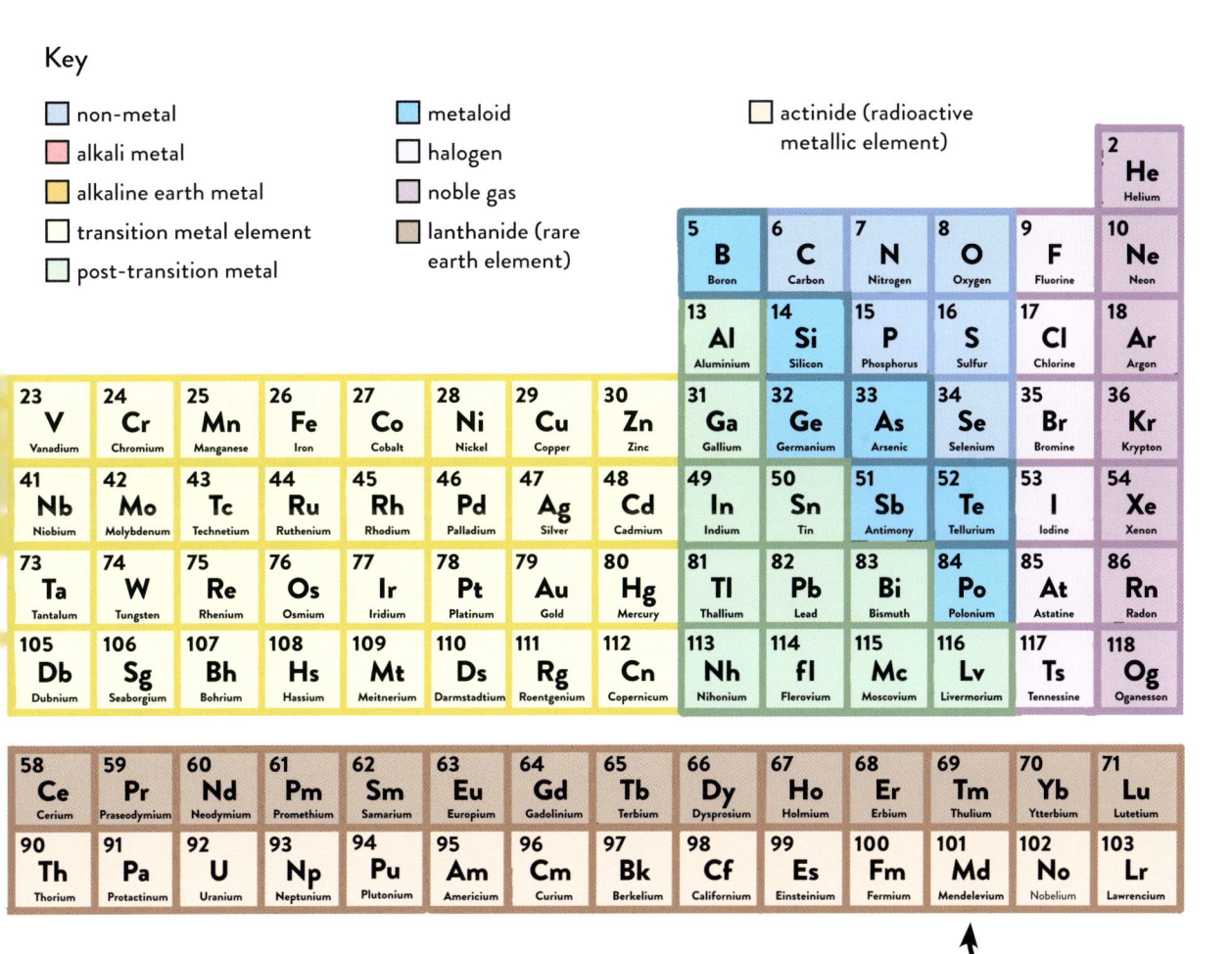

Mendeleev's periodic table, with adjustments, is still used today even though more than 50 elements have been discovered since its introduction. A new element discovered in 1955 was named mendelevium in his honor.

Pasteurization

Preserving food so that it didn't spoil was a major problem in the past, especially as there were no refrigerators. A Paris candy-maker, Nicolas Appert (1749–1841), had success in the early 19th century by sealing food in glass jars that were boiled. People didn't understand what caused food to go bad, and as a result, many suffered or died from food poisoning or contracted diseases carried in food.

In 1856, French chemist Louis Pasteur (1822–95) was asked to help a brewer whose beer kept spoiling and turning sour. Pasteur examined samples under a microscope and discovered thousands of microorganisms in the beer. He believed they were responsible for the spoiling.

Pasteur tried heating the beer to different temperatures below its boiling point to kill the microorganisms. He then cooled the liquid rapidly to stop any remaining microbes from multiplying. The technique was successful and would become known as pasteurization.

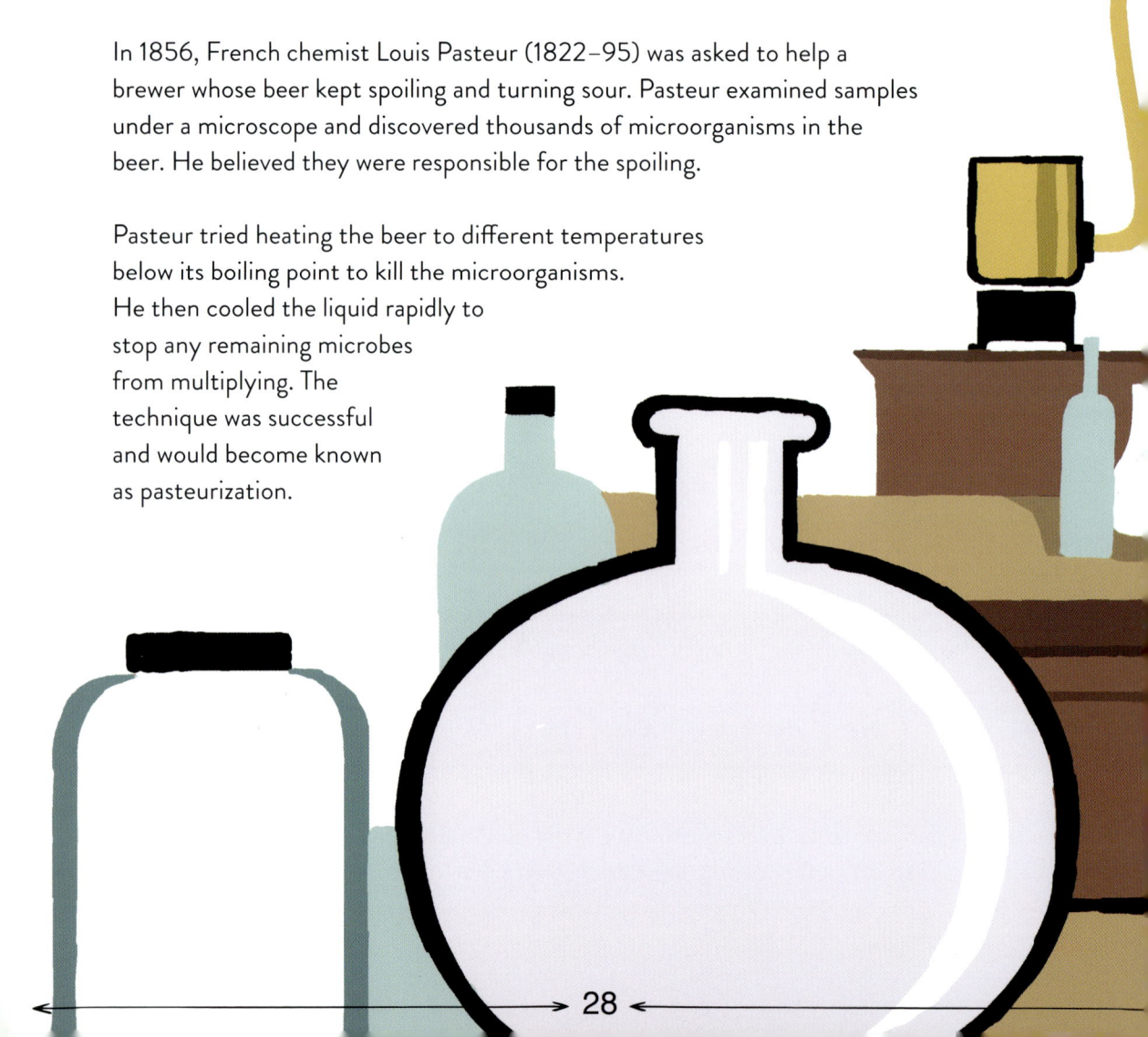

Pasteur applied his pasteurization technique to wine at the request of France's ruler, Emperor Napoleon III (1808–73). Many French winemakers were struggling with their wine turning sour before it reached customers. Boiling wine made it taste unpleasant, so Pasteur experimented. He found that heating it to between 131°F and 140°F (55–60°C) killed most of the microbes present without altering the wine's flavor.

← *Louis Pasteur*

Saving Lives

Milk, if untreated, can carry many harmful bacteria, including salmonella, listeria, and those causing the infectious disease tuberculosis. The pasteurization of milk and other dairy products would eventually save many thousands of lives.

Inheritance

Inheritance is when certain traits, such as height and hair or eye color (or in plants, the size or color of flowers) are passed from parents to their offspring. For centuries, people had experimented with breeding animals and plants, but no one understood the science behind how traits were passed on. It took the painstaking work of an Austrian monk, Gregor Mendel (1822–84), to make the first key breakthroughs.

← St. Thomas's Abbey, Brno

Mendel lived and worked at a monastery in Brünn (now Brno in the Czech Republic). He began experiments in the monastery's garden in 1856. A patient man, over a period of many years he grew a staggering 28,000 pea plants. He used a paintbrush to transfer pollen carefully from one plant to another, measured each plant for certain traits, and wrote the results down in notebooks.

He found that some traits were more dominant than others. For example, when one parent plant was tall and the other was short, their offspring were all tall. The generation after that, though, contained one short plant for every three tall plants. Mendel figured out that the less dominant trait (in this case, shortness) skipped a generation but hadn't disappeared completely.

Mendel's ideas showed how parents passed on their characteristics to future generations. This didn't apply only to plants but to all living things that have parents, including humans. Although his ideas weren't accepted at the time, in the 20th century they became the basis of genetics, the study of genes and DNA.

Gregor Mendel →

Radio Waves

Radio waves were discovered near the end of the 19th century. They were predicted to exist by Scottish scientist James Clerk Maxwell (1831–79) in the 1860s and first produced by German scientist Heinrich Hertz (1857–94) 20 years later. Like light, radio waves travel in waves through space and can be sent from a transmitter to a receiver.

The ingenious Nikola Tesla (1856–1943) from Serbia built the first radio-controlled device — a model boat — in 1898. Using a transmitter, Tesla could send wireless signals to the boat's engine and lights. It amazed people when demonstrated in New York, but radio-controlled machines wouldn't catch on for decades.

← Radio waves are a type of wave in the electromagnetic spectrum, which also includes light rays and X-rays.

Electromagnetic waves have two parts at right angles to each other: electric fields (red) and magnetic fields (blue).

In 1895, 21-year-old Italian Guglielmo Marconi (1874–1937) built a radio transmitter to send radio waves across his parents' garden. Building bigger, more powerful transmitters and antennas, Marconi sent a message across the English Channel in 1899. Two years later, he sent a signal, representing the letter S, across the Atlantic Ocean between Cornwall, UK, and Newfoundland, Canada.

Marconi's work quickly led to radio waves being used to send messages that previously would have been sent along telephone or telegraph wires. Many ships were equipped with radio transmitters that could send messages to shore or to other ships. In 1909, radio messages from a sinking ocean liner, RMS *Republic*, brought other ships to the rescue and saved the lives of over 1,500 passengers and crew.

Guglielmo Marconi ⟶

Radio Stations

Sounds, such as speech and music, were first carried by radio waves in the 1900s. The first radio stations began in the 1920s, broadcasting programs for people to listen to at home.

Radioactivity

In 1896, French scientist Henri Becquerel (1852–1908) discovered that the element uranium could give off particles and energy in the form of powerful, invisible rays. Two married scientists, Pierre (1859–1906) and Marie Curie (1867–1934), named these rays "radioactivity."

The Curies investigated pitchblende, a substance found in the ground that contains uranium but has higher levels of radioactivity than pure uranium. They reasoned that pitchblende must contain another, more radioactive substance.

In July 1898, the Curies announced their discovery of a new chemical element in pitchblende. They named it polonium after Marie's home country of Poland. Five months later, they discovered radium, another chemical element that glowed with energy in their laboratory. Radium proved to be over a million times more radioactive than uranium.

For their discoveries, which helped start a whole new branch of science, the Curies along with Henri Becquerel were awarded the 1903 Nobel Prize for Physics — the first awarded to a woman. After her husband died in a 1906 road accident, Marie Curie continued studying radioactivity. She managed to isolate pure radium and discovered that it gave off radon gas. This could be collected and its radioactivity used to combat cancer. In 1911, she became the first scientist, male or female, to win a second Nobel Prize.

Petites Curies

Marie Curie and her daughter Irène organized and helped to operate a fleet of trucks converted into mobile X-ray units during the First World War (1914–18). The trucks, which became known as "Petites Curies," ferried X-ray machines to the battlefront to help army doctors locate bullets and shrapnel in wounded soldiers' bodies, saving many lives.

Flash-Freezing

For centuries food had been preserved by cooling it in snow. This froze the food slowly, allowing large ice crystals to form inside, damaging the food. When the frozen produce was thawed, the taste and texture was different from fresh food.

U.S. naturalist Clarence Birdseye (1886–1956) studied life in the Arctic Circle. To support himself financially, Birdseye worked as a fur trader in Canada in the 1910s. There, he observed native Inuit people at work in bitterly cold conditions. The Inuit froze fish and other food within moments, plunging it into ice at temperatures as low as -40°F (-40 °C).

This flash-freezing prevented a buildup of ice crystals in the food and didn't alter the taste or texture. Back in the U.S., Birdseye experimented with machines that could flash-freeze food just like the Inuits did, but on a much larger scale.

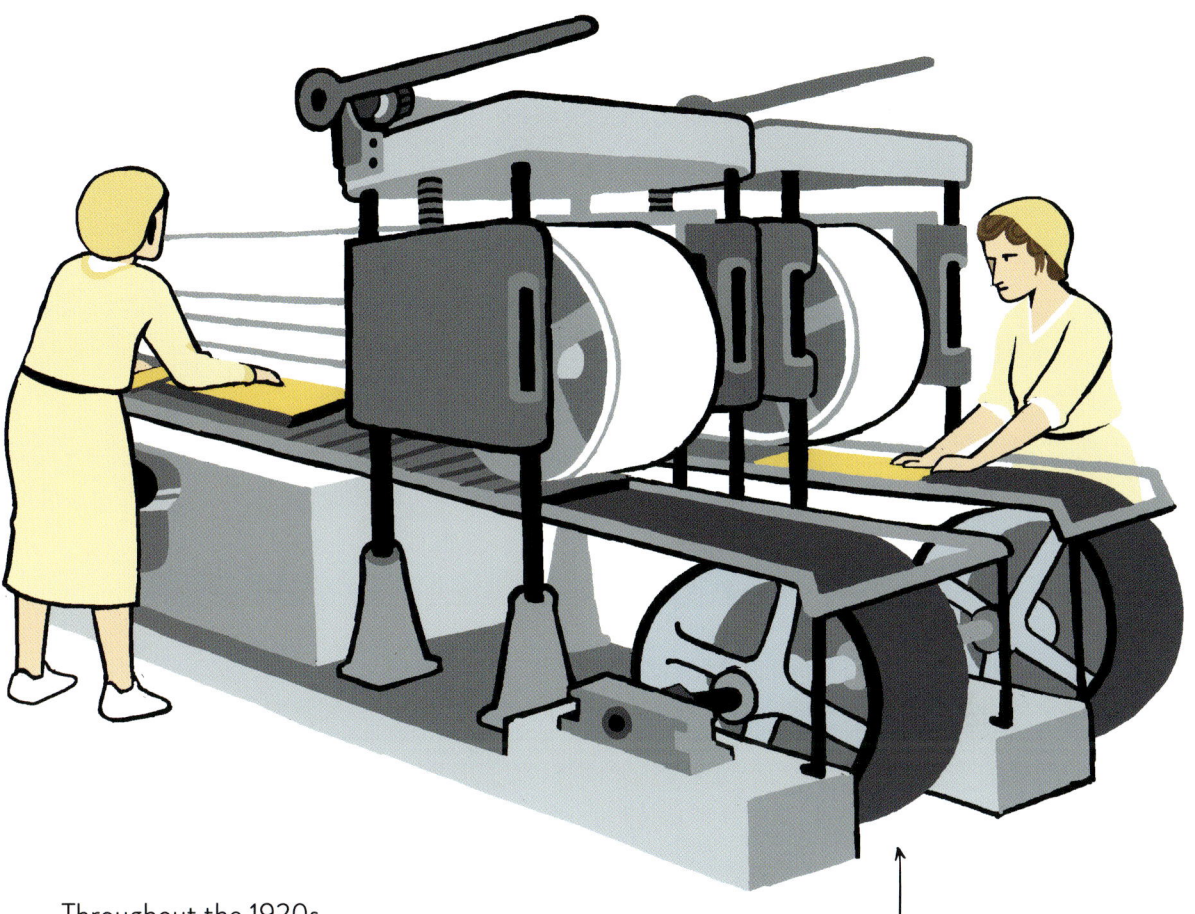

Throughout the 1920s, Birdseye improved his flash-freezing process. He invented machines that packed food into waxed cardboard boxes, which were then pressed between ultra-cold stainless steel plates to freeze them. In 1929, he sold his inventions to a big American food company but continued to develop more ideas related to frozen food.

Birdseye's flash-freezing machine

Customers found that frozen foods were tasty and nutritious. Fish, fruit, and vegetables could be bought and stored all year round, not just when they were in season. More and more homes obtained freezers, and frozen foods became extremely popular.

Continental Drift

German explorer Alfred Wegener (1880–1930) shocked the world of Earth sciences with his 1912 theory of continental drift. Wegener was fascinated by how eastern South America and the west coast of Africa looked like they would fit together snugly. He also noted how rocks of the same age and type were found on different continents, as were fossils of certain prehistoric plants and animals.

His theory suggested that the continents had all been joined together over 200 million years ago. He called this "supercontinent" Pangaea. Over millions of years, large pieces of Pangaea broke up and moved to their current positions. This explained how some ancient rocks and fossils were found on different continents thousands of miles apart.

Alfred Wegener

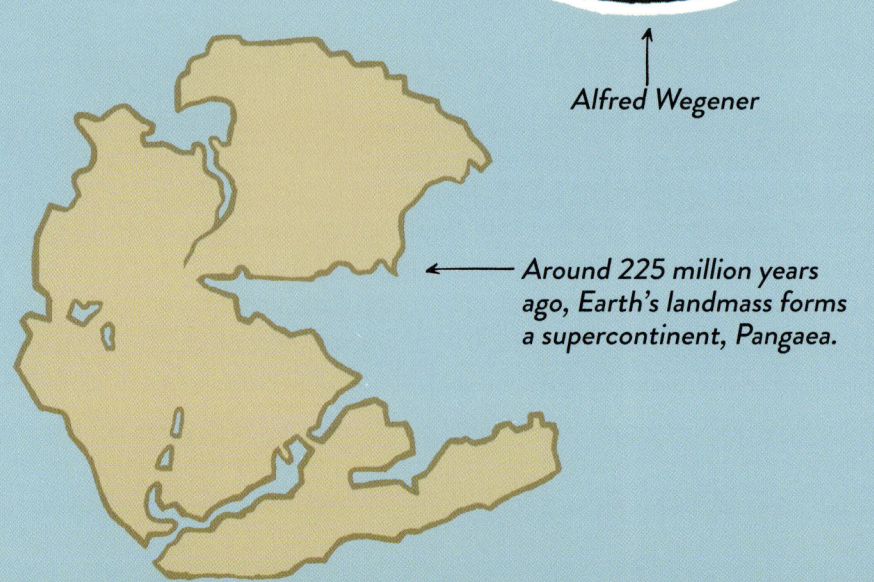

Around 225 million years ago, Earth's landmass forms a supercontinent, Pangaea.

Wegener's theory also offered a quite different explanation of how mountains form. Many people at the time thought that they were wrinkles in Earth's crust caused when Earth cooled down after forming 4.5 billion years ago. Wegener thought that mountains were much younger and caused by two continents crunching into each other and pushing rock upward.

Few scientists agreed with Wegener at the time, but his theory was largely correct. In the 1950s and 1960s, it was proved that Earth's crust is made up of seven giant rocky plates (and a few smaller ones), which slowly move around Earth's surface. These tectonic plates carry the continents apart or, in some cases, push them together. The Indian plate, for example, began pushing into the Eurasian plate around 50 million years ago, creating the Himalayan mountain range.

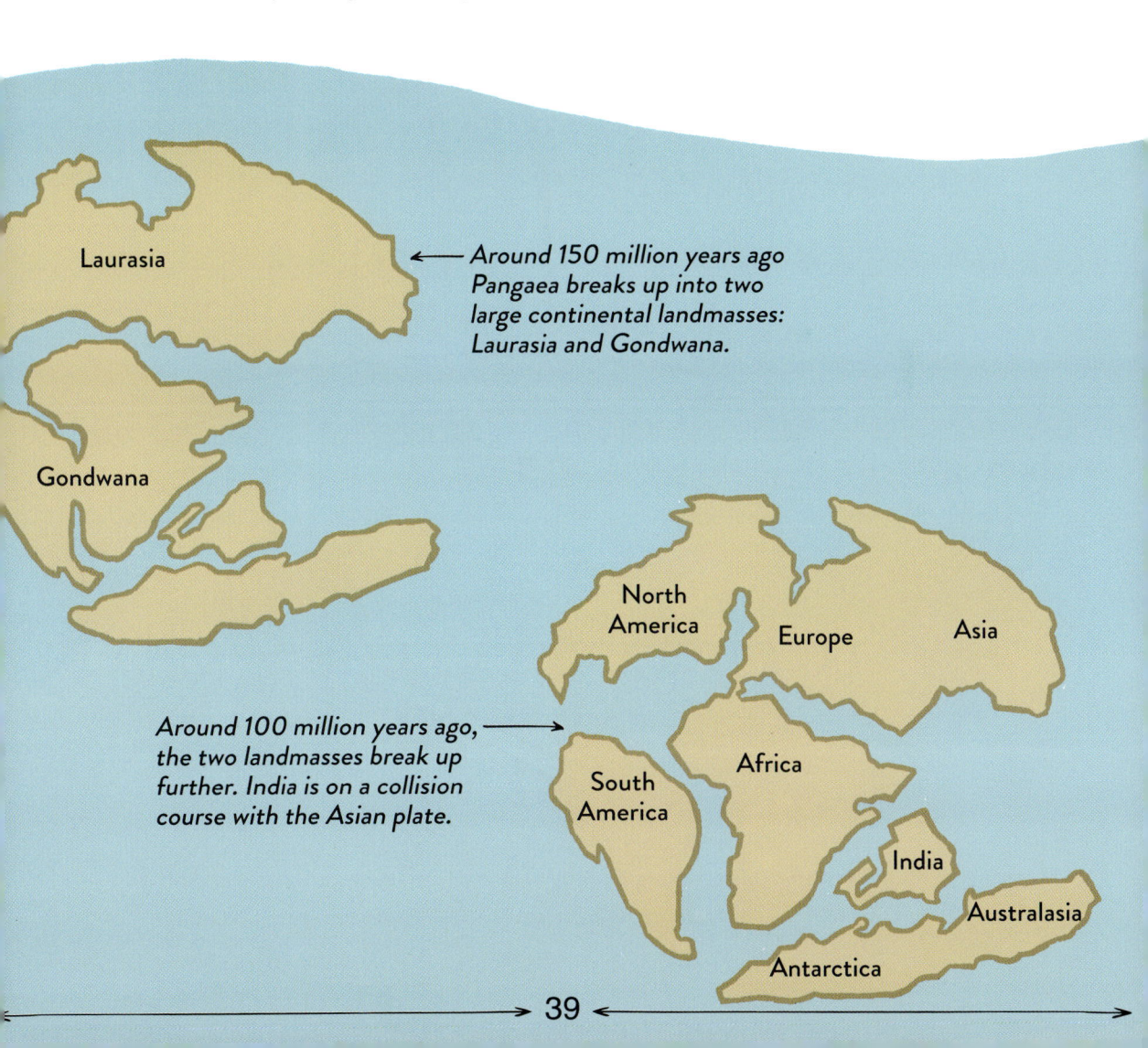

Laurasia

← Around 150 million years ago Pangaea breaks up into two large continental landmasses: Laurasia and Gondwana.

Gondwana

North America

Europe

Asia

Around 100 million years ago, → the two landmasses break up further. India is on a collision course with the Asian plate.

South America

Africa

India

Australasia

Antarctica

The Big Bang Theory

How did the universe begin? Lots of brilliant astronomers struggled with this question in the past. In the 1920s, Edwin Hubble (1889–1953) used the world's largest telescope at Mount Wilson in California to make some momentous discoveries. He found that there were lots of galaxies (collections of stars) besides our own galaxy, the Milky Way.

Edwin Hubble and the Mount Wilson observatory

Hubble also found that the galaxies were all moving away from each other. He and other scientists found out that this was occurring because the universe itself was expanding.

A young Belgian priest, George Lemaître (1894–1966), learned of Hubble's idea when he studied astronomy in the U.S. in the 1920s. Lemaître reasoned that if the universe was expanding, in the past it must have been much smaller. Working back, he figured out that it must have begun as a tiny, single point that he called "a cosmic egg." This incredibly hot and dense point suddenly expanded in a fraction of a second, creating an explosion of matter and energy

Lemaître publicized his idea in 1931. It gained the name "Big Bang Theory" in 1949. Astronomers now believe that the universe started with the Big Bang and that it occurred about 13.7 billion years ago.

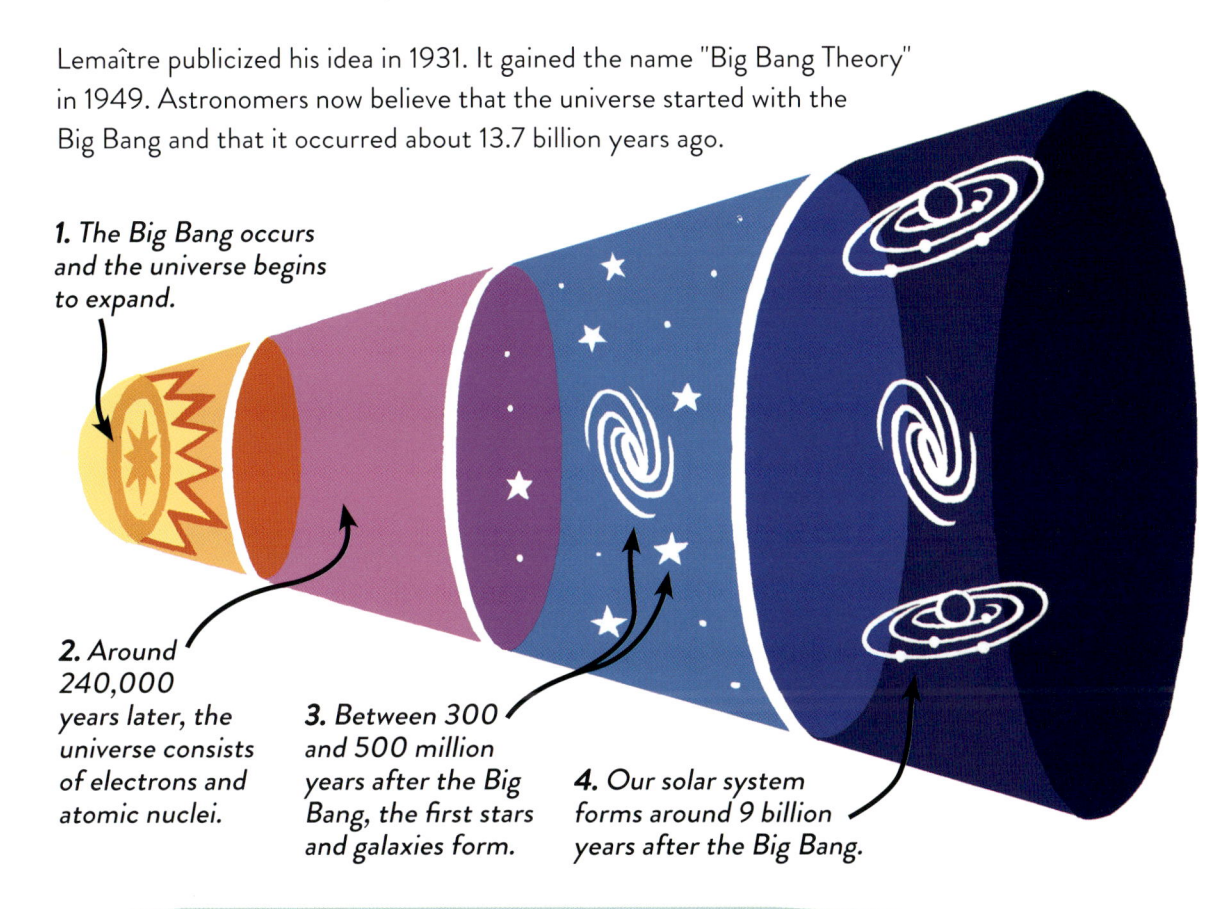

1. The Big Bang occurs and the universe begins to expand.

2. Around 240,000 years later, the universe consists of electrons and atomic nuclei.

3. Between 300 and 500 million years after the Big Bang, the first stars and galaxies form.

4. Our solar system forms around 9 billion years after the Big Bang.

Cosmic Proof

In 1964, Arno Penzias (1933–2024) and Robert Wilson (1936–) detected faint radio signals reaching their large U.S. radio telescope. The signals came from every direction in the night sky and turned out to be radiation left over from when the universe was just 380,000 years old. Called the cosmic microwave background, it helped prove that the universe did begin with the Big Bang.

Environmental Impact

People used natural ways to increase crop production for hundreds of years, such as forking animal manure into soil to improve its nutrients. By the mid-20th century, though, a large range of chemicals manufactured in factories were entering the soil as fertilizers or being sprayed on land and plants as pesticides to protect crops from insect pests. At the time, few people were thinking about the environment and how it might be damaged by such chemicals.

American nature researcher and bestselling writer Rachel Carson (1907–64) investigated the use of pesticides. She found how some of these poisonous chemicals, such as DDT, didn't disappear but spread through the soil and into water, polluting it. Carson's research also showed how the chemicals traveled through food chains as one creature eats another. As a result, dangerously high levels of harmful chemicals could build up in living things, including people.

Rachel Carson ⟶

Carson's book *Silent Spring* was published in 1962 and had a big impact. People began thinking more about the environment and questioning ways of acting that damaged it. Growing numbers of people joined ecology or conservation groups, and in 1970, the U.S. government set up the Environmental Protection Agency (EPA). Two years later, DDT was banned in the United States.

Acid Rain

In 1963, scientists studying the Hubbard Brook Forest in New Hampshire discovered that rainfall there was up to 100 times more acidic than expected. Further research showed how acid rain was the result of air pollution produced by burning coal and other fossil fuels. It was found to kill trees and to reduce the life that could survive in lakes and streams.

A plane sprays crops with pesticides
↓

Pulsars and Exoplanets

In 1967, an astronomy researcher in Cambridge, England, Jocelyn Bell (1943–), discovered regular pulses of radio waves coming from space. Each pulse came from the same place and occurred every 1.3 seconds. Bell and her colleague, Antony Hewish (1924–2021), nicknamed them LGM 1, short for Little Green Men!

Jocelyn Bell ⟶

⟵ Antony Hewish

It soon became clear that they weren't alien signals, but bursts of radio waves from an unknown type of star — later named pulsars. These small but very dense stars spin fast, making many complete turns every minute. As they spin, they send out beams of energy that sweep through space like the light from a lighthouse. Today, more than 2,000 pulsars have been discovered.

A pulsar spins ⟶

For centuries, it was thought that there were only six planets until Uranus (1781) and Neptune (1847) were discovered by astronomers. As knowledge of the universe increased in the 20th century, astronomers searched for exoplanets — planets orbiting stars other than the sun.

The first exoplanets were found in 1992 orbiting a pulsar called PSR B1257+12. They were discovered by Polish astronomer Aleksander Wolszczan (1946–) and Canadian astronomer Dale Frail (1961–) using the 1,000-foot-wide (300 m) Arecibo radio telescope in Puerto Rico — at the time the largest of its kind in the world.

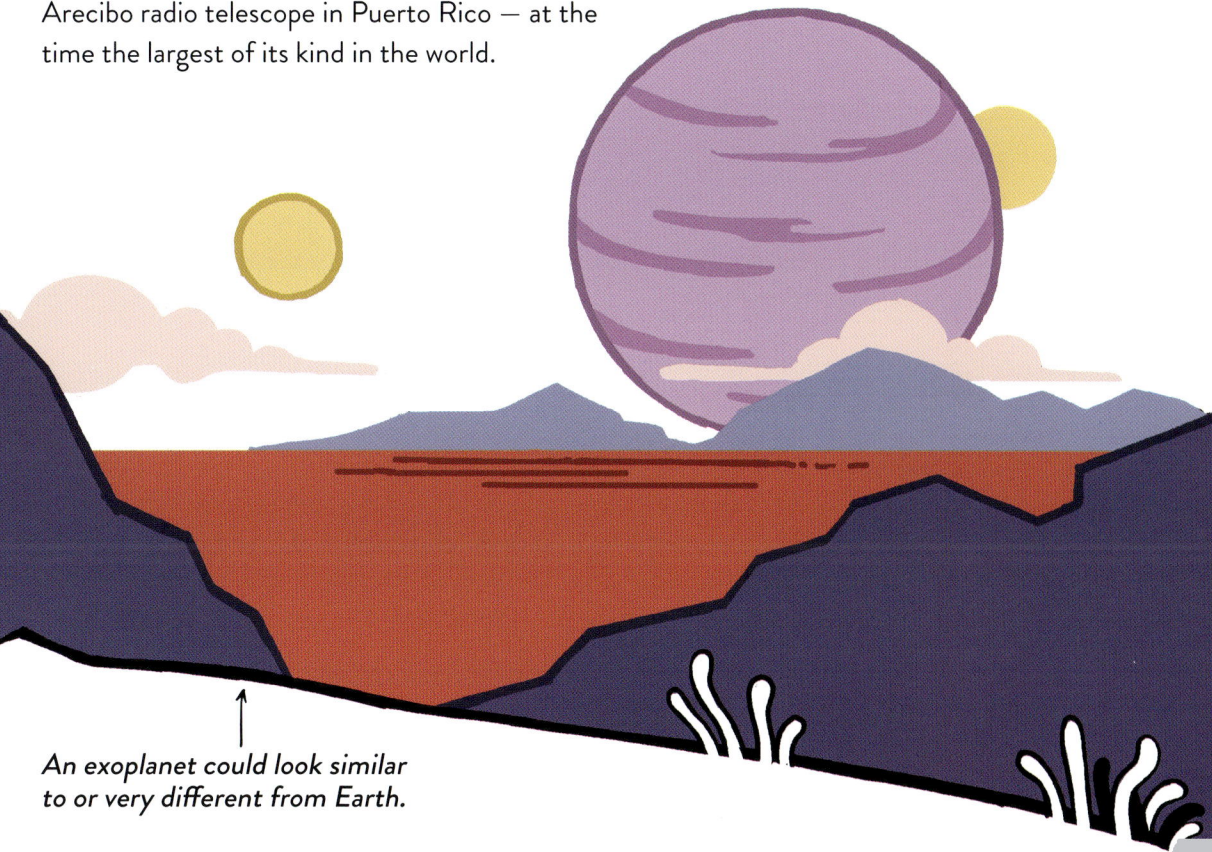

An exoplanet could look similar to or very different from Earth.

Since that time, a staggering number of exoplanets have been discovered (more than 4,000), with many more possible planets waiting to be confirmed. Astronomers are seeking out exoplanets that are warm enough, but not too warm, for life to potentially exist there. New discoveries about our own planet are exciting, but the person who finds proof of alien life may well lay claim to having made the most exciting discovery of all.

Glossary

adaptation How living things are specialized to suit their surroundings

ancestor A relative from whom you are descended, such as your father or great-grandmother

artificial Made or produced by people and not found in nature

atmosphere The blanket of gases that surround a planet

atom The basic building block of matter; atoms are made of tiny particles called protons, neutrons and electrons

bacteria A type of microscopic living thing, each made of a single cell, that exist in all environments including inside living things; some can help your body function while others can cause harm

chemical reaction A process where a set of substances undergoes a change to form a different substance

element Matter that is made from only one type of atom; oxygen, carbon, iron, gold, and nitrogen are all examples of elements

evolution The way in which living things change and develop over millions of years

extinct When a species of living thing is no longer alive on Earth

galaxy A collection of thousands, millions, or billions of stars along with planets and clouds of dust and gas, all held together by gravity

Leyden jar A glass jar lined with metal that is used to store an electric charge

mineral A solid substance that occurs naturally in the ground

molecule The smallest unit of a substance that still acts like the main substance and can take part in a chemical reaction

offspring The child or young of a species produced by parents

radioactivity The particles and rays of energy released by the atoms of some chemical elements

species A group of living things with very similar characteristics; they can breed together to make more living things of the same type

universe Everything that exists, including all the planets, stars, galaxies, and all the space in between

visible light The part of the electromagnetic spectrum that we can see

Further Information

Books

Charles Darwin: The Man, His Great Voyage, and His Theory of Evolution
by John Van Wyhe (Rosen Publishing, 2022)

Eureka: The Most Amazing Scientific Discoveries of All Time
by Dr. Mike Goldsmith (Thames & Hudson, 2016)

Isaac Newton
by Susan Meyer (Rosen Publishing, 2018)

Marie Curie: The Pioneer, the Nobel Laureate, the Discoverer of Radioactivity
by Richard Gunderman (Rosen Publishing, 2022)

Pioneers of Science and Technology
by Georgia Amson-Bradshaw (Wayland, 2018)

Women in Science: 50 Fearless Pioneers Who Changed the World
by Rachel Ignotofsky (Wren & Rook, 2017)

Note to parents and teachers: Every effort has been made by the Publishers to ensure that the websites in this book are of the highest educational value, and that they contain no inappropriate or offensive material. However, because of the nature of the Internet, it is impossible to guarantee that the contents of these sites will not be altered. We strongly advise that Internet access is supervised by a responsible adult.

Websites

www.bbc.co.uk/newsround/34486318
A roundup of exciting space discoveries made in recent times.

www.amnh.org
The American Museum of Natural History is an authority on dinosaurs and other prehistoric life.

www.thekidshouldseethis.com/post/45503937106
A great animated three-minute video explains Gregor Mendel's discovery in genetics.

www.thekidshouldseethis.com/post/evolution-101-how-natural-selection-works-nova-pbs
A five-minute video on evolution is accompanied by some great features explaining DNA and fossils.

www.youtube.com/watch?v=ijj58xD5fDI
A short animated video explains Archimedes and the discovery of displacement.

Places to visit

The Franklin Institute
Philadelphia, PA
https://fi.edu/en

California Academy of Sciences
San Francisco, CA
https://calacademy.org

Great Lakes Science Center
Cleveland, OH
https://greatscience.com

Liberty Science Center
Jersey City, NJ
https://lsc.org

St. Louis Science Center
St. Louis, MO
https://www.slsc.org

American Museum of Natural History
New York, NY
https://www.amnh

Smithsonian National Museum of Natural History
Washington, D.C.
https://naturalhistory.si.edu

Tellus Science Museum
Cartersville, GA
https://tellusmuseum.org

INDEX